The Invention of Fiction

ALSO BY RICK BURSKY

The Soup of Something Missing

THE INVENTION OF FICTION

A Chapbook

Rick Bursky

Hollyridge Press
Venice, California

© 2005 Rick Burksy

All rights reserved under International and Pan-American Copyright Conventions. Published in the United States by Hollyridge Press.

Hollyridge Press
P.O. Box 2872
Venice, California 90294
www.hollyridgepress.com

Cover and Book Design by Rio Smyth
Author Photo by Marie Astrid Gonzalez
Manufactured in the United States of America by Lightning Source

ISBN-13: 978-0-9752573-6-4
ISBN-10: 0-9752573-6-6

Grateful acknowledgment is made to the editors of the publications in which the following poems first appeared:

The Saint Ann's Review: "The Invention of Fiction"
West Branch: "The Short Season of Sleep"
Crazyhorse: "Ocular Triptych," "The Hypnology," "The History of Traitors"
Mid-American Review: Sections 5 & 8 from "The Myth of Photography"
Southern Review Review: Sections 29 & 32 from "The Myth of Photography"
Main Street Rag: Section 40 from "The Myth of Photography"

12 11 10 09 08 07 06 05   10 9 8 7 6 5 4 3 2 1

Contents

The Invention of Fiction	3
from The Myth of Photography	4
The Grandeur	25
The History of Traitors	26
The Book of My Mistakes	27
The Hypnology	28
The Short Season of Sleep	30
Sisyphus	31
Elegy Written in Four Seasons	32
Ocular Triptych	36
The Original Purpose of the Box	37
The Noise	38

THE INVENTION OF FICTION

THE INVENTION OF FICTION

1

It took seven years to teach my dog to play checkers.
Too complicated to explain here
but the one time I lost to him
instead of feeling proud I felt terrible.
Drool slid from his tongue onto the captured pieces.
This is where I admit to being small.

2

I came upon a stone brushing its teeth,
something seldom seen; stones
are loath to show desire or skill.
We can pretend this is impossible,
pretend here the truth is absent.
But there are things people see they never admit.

3

An oak in bloom at the bottom of the sea.
Dark water flowing through its branches.
Because you've never seen it
doesn't mean it's not there.
This is why fiction was invented,
to do the dirty work of belief.

from THE MYTHY OF PHOTOGRAPHY

1

When a photograph has something
to say it stares at you,
pulls at your eyes; stare back
and risk a long painful headache.
This explains why so many people leave
photography exhibits in need of an aspirin.
Photographs think people are cowards
the way they enter then exit a room
only to rearrange the emptiness.
The exceptions are yellowed photographs
nailed to walls in abandoned barns.
They believe they've found heaven,
nothing but dust and spiders and shafts
of sunlight when another plank of wood
gives up it's place in the wall.
Photographs, fortunately, never hold grudges.
This is what makes them better than people.

3

Along with other primitive tools
early evidence of photography was found
in a Neanderthal-era cave in the Pyrenees Mountains.
The discovery was made public seventeen years
after the findings and were released
in an article written by Dr. Murray Wasloff
of the State University of New York at Buffalo.
The article explained that the idea
of monastery was also created,
somewhere in that dark,
when a frightened man
cupped his hands like a cave
and into them blew warm breath.
There was no evidence to suggest
a successful exposure, this would come
tens of thousands of years later.

4

It's a method of inspecting the world.
That's you, the little boy pointing to the accident.
You're also the parent whispering
it's not polite to look.
Before we talk, I first promise this,
each photograph exists in the world just as presented.
The only information I might withhold is location.
Geography is another man's story.
What I'm about to share is a story of images,
a story of what, not the excuse of where.
I prefer to tell this story in silences.
I prefer you wrote the narrative of your choosing in the margins.
Each story can be told several ways, each would be true.
Your version of my story is the one of interest.
If a cat has nine lives what is the life expectancy of silver?
Film is animal, vegetable and mineral.
I won't tell you a secret, I'll show you one.

5

The only man to photograph
George Washington was killed
preparing flash powder in the basement of a church.
The explosion ignited a fire.
The church was destroyed.
Not one photograph of George Washington survived.
The need to immortalize, create
a catalog for history, disguise catastrophe
as art—perhaps it was nothing more
than elevating the craft of finger pointing
to something smooth and sweet as refined sugar.
Blowing magnesium powder into an alcohol flame
created an intense flash lasting an eighth of second.
Later flash powders where mixtures
of magnesium and potassium perchlorate.
The similarities between
flash powder and gunpowder
are a coincidence of intent.
If photography wasn't discovered
it would have invented itself.

8

According to the New York City Police
cameras were used as murder weapons
eight times between 1957 and 1979,
no other details. My guess,
single lens reflex cameras gripped
by a telephoto lens, swung club-like.
The cameras must have sustained
damage, though repairable.
"I closed my eyes, pressed the shutter
release, cameras know what to do,"
quote from a famous photojournalist.
The implication, cameras are responsible.
Mine are kept in a wooden cabinet
with frosted glass doors, privacy insists
the lens stay covered.

In three counties, two in New York,
one in Louisiana, it's a felony to bury a corpse
with a photograph in the coffin. Louisiana 1908,
the only prosecution for this was thwarted
when Cyrus Monteiro demanded four dollars
to retrieve a coffin, two for re-burying.
If his shovel broke the county had to replace
it with the shovel of his choosing.
No photograph exists, just a narrative
in a legal journal describing Cyrus Monterio
on the courthouse steps, unkempt gray hair,
overalls, leaning on his shovel
—that the district attorney noted was already cracked—
the judge were a starched white church-shirt dismissed
the case because Cyrus Monteiro couldn't be paid.

9

A man stands with a Shetland Pony
on a Coney Island street corner, waiting
for whatever a man with a pony waits for.
Can I sit on the pony, a little boy asks his mother.
This might not be what the waiting is for,
but the man, just the same, takes a dollar from the mother.
The little boy sits on the pony. The year is 1909.
The next day the man returns with the pony
and because a little boy can't sit on a pony forever,
brought a camera with him.
This is how photography became
as important to childhood as it was to war.
Within three years there were ninety-seven
Shetland Pony photographers
from Providence, Rhode Island,
to Washington D.C. and The Fraternal Order
of Shetland Pony Photographers was formed.
Seasonal pricing guidelines were created.
A fourteen point code of conduct was written.
Number seven: no child under eleven
years of age should be denied sitting
on the pony even if parent has no money,
a photograph isn't required.

This is all I know about The Fraternal Order.
Rosalinde Dias Vas' great grandfather was a member.
We sat cross-legged on her bed as she opened the box.
Inside, a photo of a boy and girl,
and the remains of the camera,
cracked mahogany frame, bellows
in black pieces fine as salt.
The lens to my eye, the world upside down.

10

The Traveling Brotherhood of Postcard Photographers
was created in 1936 France. The result of tourism,
one of photography's original benefactors, The Brotherhood
boasted forty-four members. All of them traveled
on bicycle, collapsible camera and film
in the front basket, tripod lashed over the rear tire.
Hotels, cafes, train stations, even prostitutes
were celebrated on postcards. Mail carried them
around the world, making these the first
photographs to enjoy an international audience.
By 1942 war reduced membership to twenty-two.
Three original members were killed in early
fighting, three went to concentration camps.
The last person to officially join
the Brotherhood after 1941
was eighteen year old Helene de la Costa.
Notoriety might have surrounded her,
the only woman in the Brotherhood,
but war prohibited such indulgences.
As a young girl, she learned
photography from her father,
who spent the war flying
with the Free French Air Force.

Before fear gives way to confusion, how long
does a man stare at an image?
Postcards flourished under Nazi occupation
—German tanks and regimental flags
in front of French landmarks, imagery as jingoism.

Helene de la Costa's postcards were popular enough
for Nazi soldiers to ask for her autographs,
and carry the tripod and canvas film bag.

Unknown to the Nazis, the subject matter
was dictated by the American Eighth Air Force.
Her postcards were important
to bomber mission briefing.
Afraid of compromising her,
commanders prohibited crews
from carrying them on missions
or sending them home until the war ended.

11

After hiding for seven hours behind a water heater
a man sneaks along a dark corridor. A key
from under the tongue unlocks the third door on the left.
Inside, he lowers his pants, squats, removes
from his anus a small camera smeared with Vaseline.

Pasadena, California, thirty-eight years later.
Bloated with cancer, the man lays in bed.
In nine days he will be dead.
Sleep becomes blasphemy.
The insignificance of walls
is finally apparent. The taste of soil
won't leave his mouth; "…your imagination"
his wife repeats, "your imagination." A postcard
from an old friend contains the photograph,
now declassified, from that night.

The camera returned to the cavity, he leans
against the water heater's asbestos blanket,
sleeps a few hours before walking out
among the workmen in the morning.

16

Depth of field, the distance you walk
home without bus fare;
depth of field, the distance Jesus' breath
floated on the final cold morning,
a collection of possibilities and its wooden box;
how far apart your eyes are.
Cigar smoke creates depth of field,
cigarette smokes doesn't.
The length of stain
tires leave on asphalt
when brakes are slammed
to unsuccessfully avoid a collision
is depth of field. A man
was sitting on a boardwalk bench
cutting wedges from a grapefruit with a pocketknife.
Sticky juice running down his hand.
He told me he was a fine art photographer
who only photographed hubcaps.
Licking the side of the blade
he cut his tongue and walked away,
blood dripping from his chin.

17

Reciprocity failure, the distrust
between science and religion,
the aftertaste of regret.
Passport photos are often the bearers
of bad news, reciprocity
failure is the explanation.
The cure for insomnia.
When you imagine hearing
sirens at midnight.
The give-and-take
between the past and the future
is not the present.
Seventeen years after
he took the job selling cameras
he continued to say it was temporary.
It no longer mattered
that he only shaved twice each week.

18

Circle of confusion, the oath
physics swore long before;
the promise we put to use
that strains us. Without
the circle of confusion
the audacity of image
would remain Braille.
The bad weather of quiet
on the outskirts. In front
of the blackboard,
between the shirt's sweat-stained armpits
he attempted, again, to explain
the science of focus,
abruptly stopped, and removed
a small paper from his pocket.
I could see his lips move
as he read to himself. Without
a word he left the classroom
leaving particles of chalk
sparkling through the sunlight
as they floated to the floor.

27

The way a cloud removes its sky.
The instant the glass, dropping
to the floor, falls away
from the water.
Disrobing in the small room
that's what it feels like.
Walking the short distance
to the pose she wears a towel.
A photograph of a naked woman
is a misunderstanding.
For ninety dollars an hour
it doesn't matter,
one hundred twenty-five
if the legs are open.
The craft of nakedness
—it's not undressing,
it's emptying.

29

The Warner Barrack's Photography Club
met in the mess hall, the second Thursday
of each month, eight at night.
Half the members were soldiers,
mostly tank crews, and one medic
who worked in the small hospital;
the rest, wives of career soldiers
and two high school girls whose
fathers were colonels.

I was the only infantryman,
in the field the weight of a camera
was carried at the expense
of candy bars, another cardboard box
of bullets, poncho or water. The weight
of necessity is unforgiving.

The coffee was free.
A mason jar collected change
for potato chips and pretzels.
Cameras on sale at the post exchange
were listed on green mimeographed paper
beside magazines and books
members wanted to trade.

Everyone brought a photograph.
One woman forgot hers,
described it instead.
A line of tourists wait
to look through the glass door
of the house where the Germans
surrendered to Napoleon.

Below, on the river,
a black sailboat is towed.
The white sky needs darkroom help.

I didn't ask anyone their name.
The next day I was being sent to Vicenza, Italy.
On the floor next to my bed,
my bag was already packed.

30

A camera hanging from the shoulder
of a monkey thirty feet above in a tree,
I couldn't tell its condition.
Only a kilometer from our base camp,
the jungle tightened around us.
I asked the lieutenant if I could borrow binoculars.
I was curious. Sergeant Ballogg
answered for the lieutenant,
pushed me forward with his rifle butt.

How long did someone search for that lost camera?
Or perhaps it was simply abandoned,
unlike water and bullets, a camera
contributes little to survival.
Without thinking I reached to the bottom
of my pack to feel my camera wrapped
in an extra pair of socks.
Someplace else, we might have had different
understandings of necessity,
but here is was simple, dry socks.

33

The average number of photographs
a death row inmate tapes to their wall is twenty-three.
There are at least three photographs
in an adult American's wallet.
In Madison, Wisconsin, a judge sentenced
a photograph of his daughter to six months in jail.

Photographs are not industrialized voodoo dolls, talismans,
or a comment on the unreliable biology of memory.
Photographs are surrogates, champions
of the one-way conversation with the past.

The man with Alzheimer's was given a gift,
a frame with a photograph
of a man and woman holding hands
as they walked along a shore.
The framed photograph sat on a bookcase
until he saw it in thirteen frames in a store.
After that, he moved it to the piano.

41

Slips of light from the window
were weakened by a sky growing thicker
with clouds. I raised the camera to my eye,
narrowed the depth of field
until the people behind her dissolved
into smudges. Her face filled the frame.
Viewfinders give the world a theatrical quality.
Each twitch, word and movement pulled flesh,
assembling and disassembling her.
Face muscles, unlike other muscles,
attach to flesh, not bone.
The face is the heart of narcissism.
The face is a transient form of identification.
The face is a dilemma.
I was a portrait photographer, I know.

A Caesar salad with two plates,
the waitress put it on the table between us.
She lifted her hands to cover her face.
This is when I discovered the face is earth,
the hands are heaven. Every portrait
since then, hands covering the face.

43

To bury his dog, a man digs a hole in his yard.
Two feet down finds a camera, and inside the camera, film.
He develops it and discovers a photograph
of man digging a hole to bury a dog.
Waist-deep in the earth,
his t-shirt sweat-stained and dirty,
baseball cap tilted back on the head; leaning
on a shovel, not posing, catching a breath.
Behind the man, the growing mound of soil.
The dead dog on a blanket, mouth open,
tongue hanging over the teeth.

The man who found a camera
while digging a hole to bury his dog
puts the photograph in an envelope,
the envelope in a drawer.

So, this is how it starts? He ponders the differences
between curiosity and coincidence.
There aren't as many as you think.

There should be a catalog of every photograph,
on the back of each a small explanation.
How helpful, he believes, for anyone who finds a photograph.
They could send a photocopy or brief description
to the catalog keeper and for a nominal fee
learn its history. Scar tissue,
that's what many are, or fireflies,
a jury of mutes hoping to be noticed.
He begins to label manila folders.

The next day he places an advertisement
in ninety-seven newspapers
asking that photographs be sent
to a post office box in Far Rockaway, New York.

I didn't want to respond to the advertisement.
But there was a photograph of a woman
wearing a thick bathrobe sitting on a swing.
Behind her a man in a sweatshirt.
Though not the last photograph
of my mother and father, one of my favorites.
Chemotherapy has left my father bald.
In my neatest handwriting, I practice writing
in three months he will be dead.

44

Creation leans against the wall
smoking a cigarette. Creation's partner,
Necessity, sits on the sidewalk reading
a week-old newspaper for the seventh time.
Both are ushers waiting
at the door. Inside
Ambition scraps greed from its cheeks,
Memory sticks its long tongue into the glass
for the last lick of gin,
and Image, on the stage,
disrobes for the camera.
But the photographer doesn't look up.
He sits at the bar sucking a wedge
of lemon and playing solitaire.

THE GRANDEUR

Stew simmered on the stove.
The last of the sun could be seen
in the dusty dinning room mirror,
even in the water glasses on the table.
On the patio, a bare-chested man did pushups.
In the bedroom, a woman darkened
her eyes with mascara.
Later that night, as streetlights burned through fog,
a little girl asked "why are the planets so low?"
How long could it continue?
No one knew, not even if the phone rang
or if an old friend joined them for dinner.
These were the days, fragile as ours,
when a moth's delicate damage
could be cause for concern.
The next morning someone looked
through a window and saw
two dogs laying on the bed
beside their master's dead body.

THE HISTORY OF TRAITORS

Every army has its traitors. The night before battle
Caesar's cousin dulled the edges of swords.
Embarrassed, Caesar expelled him.
Frank retribution followed later
—a black ball of maggots and flies
on the side of the road. The cousin's severed head.
No mention of what to do with this information.
Hesitation is an indictment;
a coin that flips an extra time can be accused.
God is the original traitor,
ask the defeated facing the firing squad.
Late in the cold war, the United States Army coated spoons
with an undetectable chemical
that turned orange under ultraviolet light
if exposed to an enzyme produced by stress.
The theory was that it would be present in traitors.
It is believed that seventy-two
of these spoons were placed
in army mess halls in Korea.
An army counterintelligence manual observes
that traitors smile more than other soldiers.

THE BOOK OF MY MISTAKES

When I was learning to shoot
a rifle in the army I killed
a lieutenant. His left arm twitched
as they tried to stop the bleeding.
Killing him was not a mistake.
It was an accident.
The difference is important.
My thumb bumped the trigger
as the lieutenant inspected the barrel.
I thought the rifle was empty,
this is noted in the book without commentary.
I carry the book with me everywhere,
concise confessions, hundreds of them.

Sometimes I read the book to myself,
always while drinking
expensive Cabernet Sauvignon
and smoking a Cuban Monte Cristo.
Yes, my ego is fragile.

Three books taped together,
pages warped by water,
secured with a length of leather
—some believe the book is a sign of illness.
I am more courageous than you,
that's all that it means.

Not putting a coin in a parking meter
before running into the laundry
to pick up my shirts—that, too,
is listed in the book. Strange as it seems,
my other parking tickets are not included.

THE HYPNOLOGY

I

A man sits on a bus bench and flips a coin.
It's just after midnight.
The next bus won't arrive for hours.
To keep the cold air off his throat
he buttons his shirt to the top.
He runs his hand over his wrinkled pants leg
like a blind man smoothing
a crumpled note to read the Braille.
This has nothing to do with a bus.
The streetlights are lost planets;
flies are moons.
Heads, return home.
Tails, remain at the bus bench.
The traffic signal clicks three time before changing.
Once, he got into bed without
even removing his shoes.

II

A soft blue light sweeps the kitchen
from a television beside a sink
filled with soapy water.
On the television, two women are riding a train.
After three hours of not being able to sleep
she washes dishes, glasses, and two days' silverware.
She imagines the two women on the television
can see her t-shirt and underwear.
The television is mute;
she doesn't want to hear what they say about her.
A siren in the distance.
A opossum in the shadow of a garbage can.
The dishes are clean.

III

A man sits on the curb smoking a cigarette
while she sleeps; raspy inhales, long exhales,
a forefinger against a thumb
when he flicks a butt into the street
before pulling another from the emptying pack.
She wakes to walk the dog
when the moon is between
a streetlight and a tree.
Her white robe billows in the breeze,
collapses, glows in the chill.
The dog sniffs at the man
in his smoky gray cloud.

There is so little to say.
Isn't this the best use of night,
to make us afraid, make us uncomfortable,
make us stare at the ceiling until morning.
Is sleep a skill or a prize?

IV

Now let me address you, dear reader,
reading in your car, only lifting your head
when you hear the front door open
and see her coax the dog along the driveway.
Are you embarrassed like the man who can't explain
his presence in a neighbor's dream?

THE SHORT SEASON OF SLEEP

A zookeeper carried a bucket of raw meat
into the lion's cage, then yawned, sat down
and began to doze. The lion was snoring,
its tail sweeping the ground in a dream.

The bank robber fell asleep at the wheel of his getaway car.
The money in the paper bag next to him closed its eyes.
Not even the dentist could resist, eventually resting
his head against the face of a slumbering patient, the small
drill left to twist harmlessly in the cavern of the mouth.

The sleepiness was contagious, drifting from one heavy eyelid to another.
The last thing anyone remembered were the voices of people
singing lullabies as they strolled arm-in-arm through the town.
Not wanting to wake his passengers, the deaf bus driver waved
and didn't sound his horn as he drove past the choristers.

No one knows what music the bats made that night
as they rose from their cave into the quiet sky
and chased a somnambulist walking along the river.

This was how the short season of sleep came and we discovered
the only difference between sleep and death was the waking up.
The next day this was discussed by everyone except the schoolteacher,
who remained at the desk in front of the classroom, her head tucked
into the fold of an arm, her blond hair moving with the breeze.

SISYPHUS

Before he brushed his teeth,
before breakfast, even before
tending the gray cat
he swept the stretch of road
in front of his house, the stretch
that rose from the flatter ground
south to the beginning of the forest
—though traffic seldom passed
and only the occasional jackrabbit stopped to stare.
Every man has responsibilities is what he thought
as he pushed away the blankets. It was dark
but wouldn't remain dark forever.

A shotgun's coarse explosion,
the crunch of gravel
under tires on the postman's truck,
the pungent stench of burning manure
—it was never far away
on the other side of the trees.
A scythe with a polished oak handle
leaned against a door.
When the grass reached his knees
that's how he would cut it
a month of afternoons.

ELEGY WRITTEN IN FOUR SEASONS

Winter

Before the cousins played softball
in the field, one of the uncles pitching
so each swing was successful,
before grass grew above the broken fence
and men sat on the hood of a car drinking beer
—the original color was white, it required no adjectives,
and was easy to see a spider walk across.
A boy with new earmuffs is first
to walk across the snow covered field
writing his name in the snow
with the yardstick from behind the basement door.
Soon the sky will tire of being black and blue
and bags of seed will be dragged from the shed.
Winter, the ghost of every season,
when everyone pretends
"coffin" is not another word for cradle.

Spring

In the early morning, windows wide
to the smell of the garden;
she sat on the bed painting her toenails,
sheets careless across her thighs,
comfortable in the season of her nakedness,
the season of anything possible.
It was probably a Sunday
and if it wasn't it should have been.
Sun darkens the flesh,
sweat sweetens it.
Later, she'll blame herself,
should have caught the faint odor
of a woman beginning to bury herself
long before her death.
Only spring makes a history
out of a woman painting
her toenails, a history
out of foreign music playing on a radio,
a man in the kitchen
squeezing oranges for juice.

Summer

The premise is simple, a matter of up and down,
give and take, perhaps breaking versus repair.
The little girl flicked her wrist.
The yo-yo plunged, a sharp fall
followed by the undoing
of gravity as it climbed back up the string.
She once asked her father to time the toy,
from plummet to return, one alligator, two alligator.
So there went the summer, warmth fading into coolness,
the speed of alligators barely brushed the buffalo grass
before being jerked back to the beginning.
The neighbor's old collie snapped at fireflies
who in their spectacular instant saw the scratch of
lightning, which to a firefly is God.
The climax of memory is death; everything previous,
happenstance, a lavish understanding
of ourselves that no one else shares.
Her mother calling from the kitchen window,
the night sky tangled in the trees,
that's how she remembers it.

Autumn

Finally, after the hot afternoons of summer,
he climbed the roof to sweep away pine needles,
clearing the gutters for the coming rains.
A chill darkened the sky,
only the bones of clouds remained.
It's autumn, not winter,
that turns men into martyrs.
The windows rattle more often.
He pauses from his chores,
pulls a pack of cigarettes from a pocket,
lights one and sucks the smoke down
like a man gulps air when he doesn't know
how long he'll have to hold his breath.
Autumn, the season that is The Coffee Cup;
the season of men on roofs,
of broken bone crickets mourning their wounds;
autumn, the season between.
The windows rattle more often.
It won't last forever, not even the owls
that spend their nights laughing at us.

OCULAR TRIPTYCH

He once feared he would swallow it,
or blind it drinking coffee,
but the man with a third eye in his tongue
learned to think of the eyelid like the door
of a vault protecting a terrible secret,
or perhaps a trapdoor to a flooded basement
where old music boxes
and a pair of crutches float.

The man with a third eye in his tongue
could see his breath shaped
into words by the mouth's warm walls.
At night, he closed the eyes in his head
and opened his mouth. His third eye
blinked, caught the black snapshots
of dreams as he slept.
His mother told a doctor,
don't talk to me about mistakes.

THE ORIGINAL PURPOSE OF THE BOX

In The Museum of Antiquities,
a guard in a gray uniform stands against the wall.
Once, he heard a woman say "I don't believe."
Once, he saw a child grow frightened.
Once, the guard told a man with an old camera
on his shoulder that photographs weren't allowed.
Invention is a series of tragedies.
The original purpose of the box
was to contain the emptiness.
Though scholars once thought
it was invented as a place to hide

a length of silk, dagger
or a crucifix from a borrowed god.
In the middle of the room
is where the first box sits.
Tragedy is a series of inventions.
Each wall, the nuance of a different disgrace.
The floor, camel tongues stitched together.
The ceiling changed with the weather.
At night the guard takes the box home.
As he rides the bus it sits on his lap
as if it held his lunch or a gift.

THE NOISE

Halfway across the room, she realized
she couldn't hear her footsteps on the wooden floor.
At first she thought it was because she painted her toenails red.
But this was the color she wore when she ran from his house,
her footsteps louder than crows in the trees.

The captain of a ship in the harbor was woken.
The noise could have been the slap of waves
or the deck watch knocking at his door.
From his porthole he saw a light
in a house above the docks.

In the morning the ship would weigh anchor
and sail east, this much she knew.
She closed the light, returned to bed and hopefully sleep.
The click, click, click of the ceiling fan
cooled what remained of the night.

www.ingramcontent.com/pod-product-compliance
Lightning Source LLC
Chambersburg PA
CBHW022346040426
42449CB00006B/747